102

School

Cafeteria

Jokes

Morgan

Troll

Library of Congress Cataloging-in-Publication Data

Matthews, Morgan.
    102 school cafeteria jokes / by Morgan Matthews.
        p.   cm.
    Summary: A collection of jokes about school cafeterias and the
foods served there, including "Why were ducks in the cafeteria? The
students were having soup and quackers for lunch."
    ISBN 0-8167-2611-6 (pbk.)
    1. Wit and humor, Juvenile.   2. School lunchrooms, cafeterias,
etc.—Juvenile humor. [1. Jokes.   2. Riddles.   3. School
lunchrooms, cafeterias, etc.—Wit and humor.   4. Food—Wit and
humor.]   I. Title.
PN6163.M28   1992

This edition published in 2002.

Printed in Canada.

10 9 8 7 6 5

What do math teachers do in the cafeteria?

They divide their lunches between them.

What kind of sandwich sinks to the bottom of your stomach?

A sub sandwich.

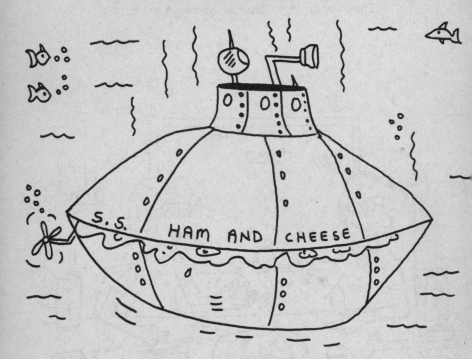

Why does the person in charge of school never skip lunch?

It's his principal meal.

Why did the student throw his lunch in the garbage?

It was nothing but junk food.

What do you get if you cross a lunch box and a school book?

Food for thought.

What snack food tells dumb jokes?

Corny chips.

Why wasn't the rocket in the cafeteria?

It went home for launch.

What side dish do miners eat with lunch?

Coal slaw.

What is a driving instructor's favorite lunch?

Park chops.

Who saved the cafeteria from the bad guys?

The hero sandwich.

What kind of frankfurter shivers a lot?

A chilidog.

What did the bread say to the margarine?

Don't try to butter me up, pal!

What do joggers do at lunch time?

They eat and run!

What dessert is cold and rings?

An ice-cream phone.

Why did the student bring scissors into the cafeteria?

So he could cut the lunch line.

When does a sandwich ask a lot of questions?

When it's made of why bread.

What kind of snack food does somersaults?

Potato flips.

What do you get when a ghost flies into the cafeteria at lunch time?

A food fright.

Where do baby cows eat their lunch?

In a calf-e-teria.

What kind of sandwich is a coward?

A chicken sandwich.

Who can work magic in the cafeteria with a skillet?

A frying sorcerer.

What kind of cookies do birds eat at lunch time?

Chocolate-chirp cookies.

Which kitchen utensil has a pilot's license?

The flying pan.

Why don't bananas wear shoes?

They already have slippers on.

What's green and bores holes?

A drill pickle.

What does a baseball umpire put his lunch on?

A home plate.

What did the hamburger say to the frying pan?

Don't burn me up, pal!

Which athletes are the sloppiest eaters?

Basketball players. They dribble food all over themselves.

What do cave men like to have for lunch?

Club sandwiches.

Why did the school hire an artist to decorate the cafeteria?

They wanted the lunchroom to be a tasteful place.

How do you stop a hamburger from burning up?

Smother it with onions.

What did the cook say to the salad?

You're old enough to dress yourself.

What kind of sandwich is Dracula afraid of?

A stake sandwich.

Which condiment is used by politicians in charge of cities?

Mayor-naise.

Where do student astronauts eat their midday meal?

In the *launch*room.

What did one scrap of bread say to the other?

You're a crumby friend.

How did the gangster pay for his lunch?

He forked over the cash.

What's pink and steals food?

A ham-burglar.

What do ghost students eat at lunch time?

Boo-loney sandwiches.

What do you call stolen cafeteria food?

Hot lunches.

What kind of plates do Martian students eat lunch on?

Satellite dishes.

What did the English teacher put at the end of her sentence about the cafeteria?

A lunch period.

What snack is old but good for you?

A granny-ola bar.

What did the lunch cook say to the boiled hot dog?

I told you you'd get into hot water someday.

Why did the police arrest the hamburger?

They wanted to grill him at the station.

Where's the best place to hang soggy sandwiches to dry?

On the lunch line.

Why were ducks in the cafeteria?

The students were having soup and quackers for lunch.

What did the rich kid say when he spilled his food in the cafeteria?

Don't worry everyone. Lunch is on me.

What do little monsters like to have for lunch?

Alpha*bat* soup.

What's made of bread and works magic?

A sand*witch*.

What did the basketball player do with his doughnut?

He dunked it.

Why did the school hire a tightrope walker to prepare lunches?

They wanted the students to have a balanced diet.

What kind of locomotive do you find in the cafeteria?

A chew-chew train.

What do math teachers like to do at lunch time?

They like to count calories.

What items on the lunch menu got fired?

The vegetables. They were canned.

How did the plate get a crack in it?

It had a lunch break.

Why did the knife get in trouble at the lunch table?

It kept cutting up.

What do dance students drink to wash down their lunch?

Tap water.

How did the turkey get a stomachache?

It gobbled up its lunch too fast.

Why did the silly student eat a dollar bill?

It was his lunch money.

Why was the quarterback asked to leave the lunchroom?

He wouldn't pass the ketchup.

Why did the students sprint out of the cafeteria?

They had fast food for lunch.

What paper products always doze off at lunch time?

Nap-kins.

What did the hot dog say after it was smeared with relish?

Now I'm in a pickle.

What did the coffee beans say on Monday morning?

Oh well, back to the old grind.

What did the leopard say when he walked into the lunchroom?

Save me a spot at the table.

Why were the gangsters in the kitchen?

They were cooking up a robbery.

What does the snowman use to make sandwiches for his kids?

Cold cuts.

How did the lettuce get an "A" on the salad test?

It just used its head.

What's a grumpy salad made of?

Lettuce alone.

What salty snack food lives at the Arctic Circle?

Pret*seals.*

What kind of cheese did the basketball player put on his sandwich?

"Swish" cheese.

Why did the boy bring a canary to the cafeteria?

He wanted to have a tweet after lunch.

What did the geometry teacher have for lunch?

A square meal.

Why did the fast-food cook get his eyes examined?

He kept seeing double cheeseburgers.

What did the slice of bread say to the sweet roll?

Will you be my honey bun?

What kind of shoes do hamburgers wear?

Meat*loafers.*

What kind of drink fizzles and roars?

A lemon-lion soda.

Which day of the week is the best day to cook hamburgers for lunch?

Fry-day.

Why did the teacher give lunch a good grade?

It passed the taste test.

When did the student howl in the cafeteria?

After he wolfed down his lunch.

What did one hot dog say to the other?

Please be frank with me.

How do geese like their ice cream served?

In a *ducksie* (dixie) cup.

What's the worst kind of cake you can eat for dessert?

A cake of soap.

What do cheerleaders like to drink with their lunch?

Root beer.

What do bowlers like to eat for lunch?

Spare ribs.

What did the cole slaw say to the policeman?

You don't have a shred of evidence against me.

What pastry has a fat stomach?

A belly doughnut.

Why was the beef soup giggling?

It was made with laughing stock.

What do kangaroos like to drink with their lunch?

Spring water.

BOING!
BOING!
BOING!

Why did the silly gym teacher bring a tennis racket to the cafeteria?

He wanted to serve lunch.

What did one meat sandwich say to the other?

I don't believe you. You're full of baloney.

What do you use to glue a broken pizza?

Tomato paste.

Why did the cook try to make the cucumber laugh?

He wanted to see if it was picklish.

What do you call a dopey hamburger?

Beef jerky.

Why do hamburgers always beat hot dogs at sports?

Because hot dogs are the wurst.

What's a down-to-earth sandwich made out of?

Ground beef.

Why did Dracula visit the cafeteria?

He just dropped in for a quick bite.

What's round and found on the bottom of the ocean?

A meatball sub.

What is a pickle's marriage vow?

Dill death do us part.

Where do busy bees go at noon time?

Out for a *buzzness* lunch.

What did one glass say to the other?

Let's break for lunch.